BARBARA JONES (1912-1978) was born in Croydon, Surrey, where her family ran a high street saddlery. She studied at the Croydon School of Art and the Royal College of Art, in the footsteps of Edward Bawden, John Piper and Eric Ravilious. Like them, she was interested in the architecture, landscape and the folk and decorative arts of Britain. During the Second World War she was commissioned by The Pilgrim Trust to document historic buildings at risk from war damage. The paintings she produced were included in the landmark publication *Recording Britain* (1946-1949) and are now held at the Victoria & Albert Museum. She was a prolific illustrator of books, and wrote and illustrated several of her own, including *Follies and Grottoes* and *The Unsophisticated Arts*.

TWIT & HOWLET & THE BALLOON

Barbara Jones

Little Toller Books

The Owls lived in an oak tree called **THE PINES**.

They are a large family of uncles and aunts, brothers, sisters, cousins.
And we must not forget Grandma.

   Twit and Howlet are the youngest. They are twins. Sometimes they are
indulged and sometimes they are sat upon, like everyone else.

One day after dinner there was a tremendous argument about a cat trap.
Owls and cats had once been enemies. But now the trap had little use in the Owl
household, the older Owls struggled to remember what it looked like.

'It was made of wire and shaped like a lobster pot.'

'It was made of wire all right, but it was a sort of tunnel-shape. You'd never
get a cat into a lobster pot.'

'You're both wrong—it was square. I'll get it up from the cellar.'

'It isn't in the cellar. Hubert is growing plants in it.'

'You are all wrong,' announced Grandma. 'I bought it and I should know. It is
mouse-shaped, and it is in the attic.'

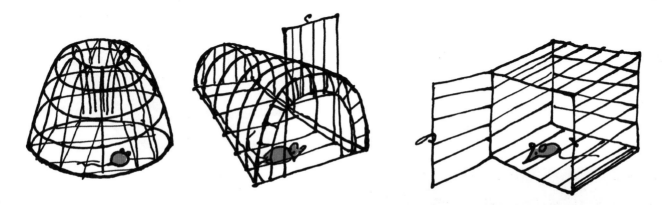

'I'll get it,' cried Twit and Howlet as one, racing up the tree. The twins loved the attic. They spent many wet days dressing up with old clothes from the trunks, and making new things out of old things put away because they might-come-in-useful-someday.

They found the cat trap behind a trunk behind a pram. Grandma was quite right: it was indeed mouse-shaped.

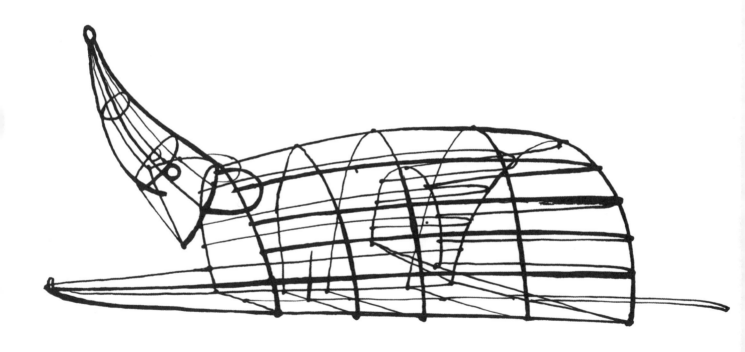

They took it downstairs, but no one took any notice. The argument had shifted to the nightly row about the correct colour balance of the TV.

Twit and Howlet soon became bored. Howlet's thoughts floated back to the trap. It looked so promising, a new treasure! There must be *something* they could do with it.

Howlet suddenly jumped up and down shouting, 'It's a balloon basket! It's a balloon basket!'

The older Owls glared at this noisy interruption.

Howlet raced into the hall, Twit followed gloomily.

Howlet was looking at a photograph over the umbrella stand. There was no doubt, this was the best picture in the house. There stood a crowd, earth-bound on the field or tree-bound in the oaks, and *there* was **THE BALLOON**, silent and free, up and away. The stripes were scarlet, the basket pale gold. They absolutely had to have one of their own.

Next morning, the twins went to the public library for books and plans and diagrams. It wasn't as simple as it seemed. They certainly had the balloon basket ready-made, but that was the least of it. Money would be needed for silk, ropes, a grapnel, burners and gas tanks. Then things had to be done to the silk. They also had to have ballast, provisions and a hoop.

They returned to the attic. There were a lot of old clothes and curtains. There were some new bits of cloth, and some of it was silk. But their vision of an elegantly pleated, white-and-scarlet balloon faded. Howlet worked out a paper pattern. They did the best with what they had. But one could easily distinguish a butcher's apron and a pirate's vest. There was only one piece of scarlet.

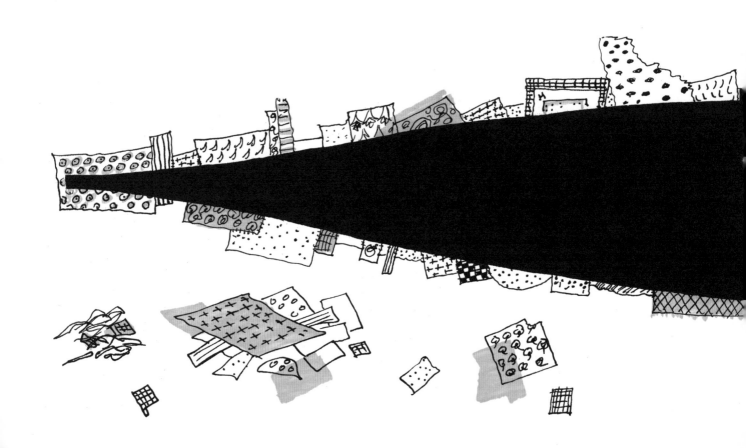

Cord for the net meant pocket money and broken claws. The burner, the hose and the tank of gas put paid to most of this year's Christmas presents.

The hoop was a hoop (too easy, thought Howlet).

Twit collected sand for ballast (and wouldn't say where from).

SAND

MORE SAND

LESS SAND

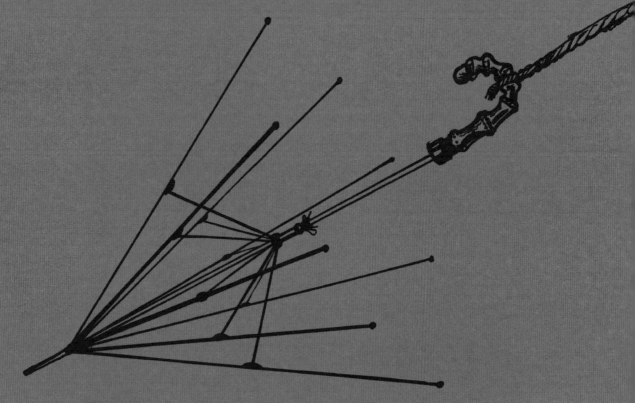

Next they shortened the cat trap, cut the top off and padded the rim with rags. They put down comfortable bits of spare lino in the bottom. An old umbrella served for a grapnel. 'Umbrellas catch in things,' Twit mused.

Thinking about what there was left to do, Howlet got depressed. 'Critical Path Analysis,' he said. Twit looked startled. 'That means we start with the longest problem first, and our longest problem is the gunge for the balloon's envelope.'

'What's gunge?' Twit asked.

'Oil, rubber or mastic,' replied Howlet, importantly.

'What's mastic?'

'Gummy stuff.'

Twit gave Howlet a withering look. 'That's the same as gunge! You are one for complicating things. . . What does it say in the book?'

'Not much,' Howlet said, beginning to read aloud: 'The balloon envelope is made of treated silk, linen or other materials.'

'Well, I know what "treating" is even if you don't,' scorned Twit. 'And it certainly isn't oil, rubber or mastic.'

The argument was stopped by Grandma.
To keep them quiet she gave Twit and Howlet
what they needed: a pot of Owl's Relish, some
cream and a glass of sherry. The twins began
mixing all this sticky stuff into the fabric of
the balloon, with ritual exclamations of 'Many
Happy Returns of the Day' and 'Let Me Get You
Another Drink'. Sadly, all the hot air escaped.

Next morning, Howlet went back to the library and then on to the Chemist's, returning with a tin of something that the books and the Librarian and the Chemist all said would be suitable.

Twit and Howlet started to treat the balloon fabric again, first with elation, then with stickiness, and finally with complete immobility. Eventually, it was all done and hung up to dry.

Envelope, basket, cords: all was ready. Nothing to get now but provisions.

Before dinner they had a long, gruesome preen using the gunge solvent the Chemist had prudently given to Howlet.

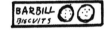

Provisions. Grandma, who had an adventurous youth, knew about these things and was having a lovely time drawing up a list of **ABSOLUTE NECESSITIES**, and next day they went with Mother to buy them. Grandma also added a present for their adventure: two very chic pairs of sun-spectacles.

LIST FOR BALLOONING

Two tins of sardines
Four tins of corned vole
A large grubcake newly baked
*A packet of mousewiches in foil for
immediate use*
Chocolate (milk and plain)
Apples, dates and bananas
Biscuits in four kinds
*Three bottles of milk in case one
breaks*
A large jerry can of water
*Two mugs, two plates, two knives,
two forks*
A box of paper handkerchiefs (large)
*Two raincoats, two pairs of
Wellingtons*
Two sou'westers, two mufflers
*One camera, one notebook with
ballpoint on string*
*Four maps, an axe, a pair of
binoculars*
Two boxes of matches
*A compass, three foreign dictionaries,
more string*

They packed everything in the cat trap.
'The *Basket*,' insisted Howlet.
'Still looks like a cat trap to me,' said Twit.

Everyone was up before dawn next day. It was a little misty, but it didn't look like there would be rain. Twit and Howlet connected the hose and lit the burner. The balloon fabric filled. 'Let go! Let go!' Howlet yelled.

'Be careful!' Mother gasped.

'They do have wings,' Grandma shouted as she cut the anchor rope.

The balloon began to rise.

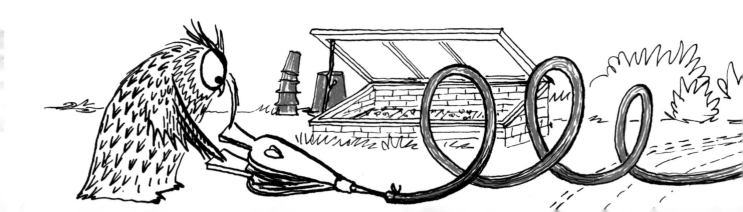

Up and up, it was not long before the land was gone and below them was the sea. What was ahead? France? Belgium? The South Pole? Would they drift off the map? It was certainly cold. They looked at the compass: they were gliding east-south-east and their speed was tremendous. They put on Wellingtons, sou'westers and mufflers. They ate a nautical tin of sardines and some biscuits.

When the sun came out they moved silently, over a warm and glittering world. They took off the mufflers and moved onto mousewiches, eating them in a trance of joy. 'Never down again!' 'To Timbuctoo!' 'Round the world we go!' But suddenly Twit sneezed. They looked down. They were moving much too fast, and a cold wind was blowing a great bank of black cloud towards them.

They saw the coast ahead. They were slowing down and began sinking towards a forest.

'The balloon is leaking!' Twit squeaked.

'Will it clear the trees?' Howlet shrieked.

They took off their hot clothes and put on their sun-spectacles.

Howlet reached for the ripcord.

'Wait! Look!' Twit gave him the binoculars. 'There's something there. Down by the village! They'll help, hang on a minute!'

Howlet looked below at the crowd of cheering owls, all waving, voices crying, 'Descendez!' 'Vite!' 'Maintenant!' 'Tirez!'

Howlet tirezed.

They came down **PLUMP**, **PLUMP**, **PLUMP**, into hundreds of eager, friendly wings.

Thank goodness they had brought the dictionaries!

The huge banner read:
GRAND BALLOON RACE
FINISHING POST

AND. . .

. . . THEY HAD WON!

They were first! Even though they were the smallest owls in the race.

What a fine day! And they were just in time for lunch—perfection!

They were led to the platform for a huge gold cup full of champagne, and then to the banquet. It was magnificent and delicious and it lasted all afternoon. Then there were speeches. The Mayor extolled their courage, their enterprise, their triumph, and ended with the story of Ballon-Sur-Somme, his glorious village, where the first owl-balloon ascent was made in 1783. . .

'I thought it was at—' Howlet began, but Twit kicked him under the table with an 'at-tish-hooo'. The Mayor hadn't heard and he went solemnly on with his speech.

That night, when the splendid festivities ended, Twit and Howlet were tucked into bed (just like in England).

In the morning, eager volunteers packed the balloon (except for souvenir snips) and all the equipment (except the milk which had gone sour) into the cat trap. They drove the twins to Boulogne and onto a hydro-wing.

But how superior the balloon was, Twit and Howlet thought. How dull the sea. They slept all the way home, but woke in time to give **THE CUP** a polish and themselves a quick preen.

They were just in time for tea. And—amazingly—to see
it all again on TV There they were, large as life with the
Mayor, **THE CUP**, and all their new friends. The twins
stood by the screen for colour comparison. They were
preened down, fluffed up. Volumes were turned, voices
raised. It was the best colour-row ever.

What a marvellous trip! How nice to be home!